THE STORY BEHIND

TOILETS

Elizabeth Raum

Heinemann
LIBRARY

www.heinemannlibrary.co.uk
Visit our website to find out more
information about Heinemann
Library books.

To order:
☎ Phone +44 (0) 1865 888066
🖹 Fax +44 (0) 1865 314091
🖥 Visit www.heinemannlibrary.co.uk

Heinemann Library is an imprint of Capstone Global
Library Limited, a company incorporated in England
and Wales having its registered office at 7 Pilgrim Street,
London, EC4V 6LB – Registered company number:
6695582

"Heinemann" is a registered trademark of Pearson
Education Limited, under licence to Capstone Global
Library Limited.

Text © Capstone Global Library Limited 2009
First published in hardback in 2009
The moral rights of the proprietor have been asserted.

Edited by Louise Galpine, Megan Cotugno,
  and Laura Knowles
Designed by Philippa Jenkins and Artistix
Original illustrations © Capstone Global Library Ltd
Illustrated by Tony Wilson, p. **5**; Phil Gleaves/Specs Art
  pp. **6**, **14**, **18**; Darren Lingard, p. **10**
Picture research by Mica Brancic and Elaine Willis
Originated by Modern Age Repro House Ltd.
Printed in China by CTPS

ISBN 978 0 431114 97 2 (hardback)
13 12 11 10 09
10 9 8 7 6 5 4 3 2 1

British Library Cataloguing in Publication Data
Raum, Elizabeth
The story behind toilets. – (True stories)
628.4
A full catalogue record for this book is available from the
British Library.

Acknowledgements
We would like to thank the following for permission to
reproduce photographs: Alamy p. **4** (© Richard Heyes); ©
Bridgeman Art Library p. **12** (Guildhall Library, City of
London); Corbis pp. **7** (© Roger Wood), **8** (© Bob Krist),
11 (© Bettmann), **13** (© Leonard de Selva), **19** (© epa), **20**
(zefa/© Mika), **27** (© Reuters/David Gray); Getty Images
pp. **15** (Look/© Franz Marc Frei), **16** (Stringer/© Jeff
T. Green), **21** (Stone/© Robert Holmgren), **22** (© Scott
Olson); © Incinolet p. **24**; © Mary Evans Picture Library
2008 p. **17**; Science Photo Library pp. **23** (© Mark Sykes),
25 (© Alan Sirulnikoff), **26** (© NASA); Shutterstock p. **iii**
(© Morgan Lane Photography); Topfoto p. **9** (© Fotomas).

Cover photograph of man's legs under toilet door
reproduced with permission of Photolibrary Group
(Blend Images).

Every effort has been made to contact copyright holders of
any material reproduced in this book. Any omissions will
be rectified in subsequent printings if notice is given to the
publisher.

All the Internet addresses (URLs) given in this book were
valid at the time of going to press. However, due to the
dynamic nature of the Internet, some addresses may have
changed, or sites may have changed or ceased to exist since
publication. While the author and publishers regret any
inconvenience this may cause readers, no responsibility for
any such changes can be accepted by either the author or
the publishers.

Contents

Some words are shown in bold, **like this**.
You can find out what they mean by
looking in the glossary.

Potty talk

▲ People usually sit down when they use European-style toilets like this one.

Whether they stand up, squat, or sit down, all people need toilets. When people eat and drink, their bodies use what they need and then get rid of the rest as waste. Liquid waste is called **urine**. Solid waste is called **excrement**.

In the United Kingdom, people say they go to the toilet, lavatory, or the loo to get rid of bodily waste. In the United States, people say they go to the restroom or bathroom. In past times, toilets were called privies. Toilets outside the house are called outhouses, necessary houses, or **latrines**. Toilets, no matter what they are called, are an important part of daily life.

▶ **This diagram shows the major parts of the body used in digestion.**

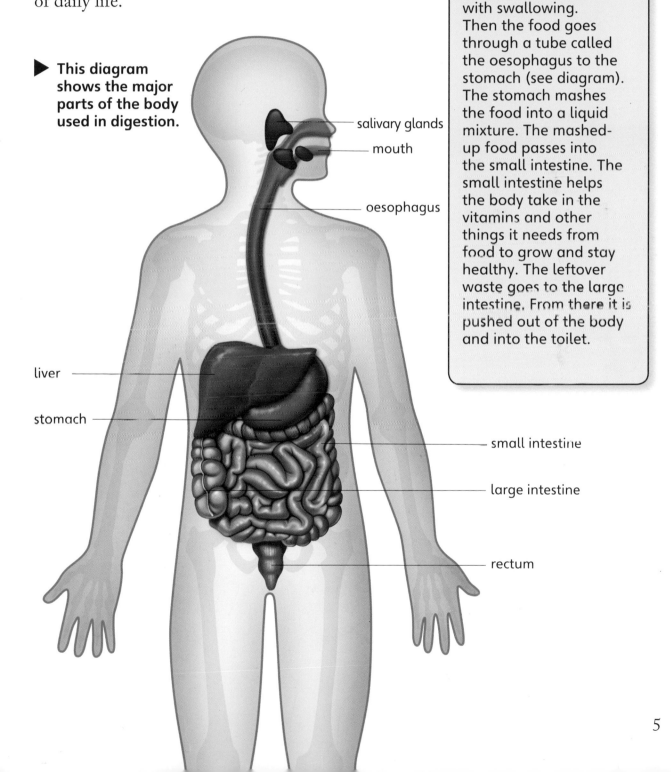

salivary glands

mouth

oesophagus

liver

stomach

small intestine

large intestine

rectum

Digestion ✓

Digestion is the process that lets the body get vitamins and energy from food. When people eat, the saliva in the mouth softens the food. This helps with swallowing. Then the food goes through a tube called the oesophagus to the stomach (see diagram). The stomach mashes the food into a liquid mixture. The mashed-up food passes into the small intestine. The small intestine helps the body take in the vitamins and other things it needs from food to grow and stay healthy. The leftover waste goes to the large intestine. From there it is pushed out of the body and into the toilet.

A short history of toilets

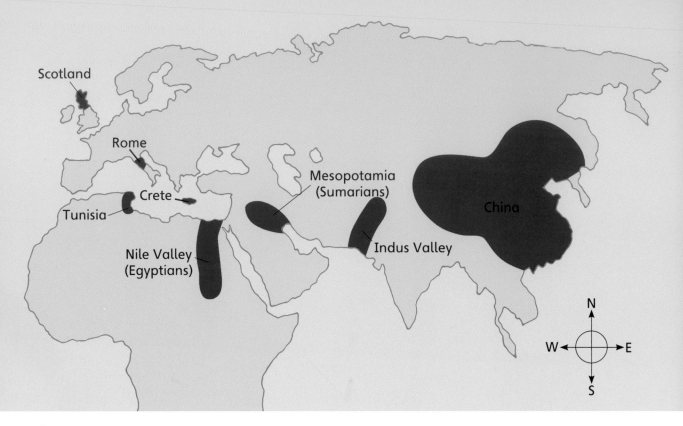

Scotland

Rome

Crete

Tunisia

Nile Valley
(Egyptians)

Mesopotamia
(Sumarians)

Indus Valley

China

N
W ← → E
S

▲ **This map shows
the places in the
ancient world that
developed toilets.**

Early people did not live in towns or villages. Instead, they camped in one place for a while. Then they moved on. They left their waste behind. As people began to live in communities, they had to find another way to deal with human waste.

At first ancient people dug holes for waste or used pots that had to be emptied. In about 2500 BCE (4,500 years ago) ancient communities in Scotland and in the Indus Valley (present-day Pakistan) used a system of pipes to carry waste outside from indoor toilets. At about the same time, the king of Sumer in Mesopotamia built six toilets in his palace.

2500 BCE
Toilets exist in Mesopotamia, the Indus Valley, and Scotland.

2000 BCE
Flush toilets are used in Crete.

3000 BCE

2000 BCE

Other ancient toilets

Toilets in ancient Egypt had a keyhole shape to make them comfortable. A pot beneath the seat was filled with sand. Human waste fell into the sand and was emptied by a servant. Later, the Romans (who lived in present-day Italy) built **sewer** systems. The sewers carried waste from toilets into nearby streams and rivers.

Flush toilets

The palace of Knossos, built about 2000 BCE (4,000 years ago) on the island of Crete, had the first toilets that flushed. Pans on the roof of the palace collected rainwater. Pipes slowly carried the rainwater to the toilets, washing away waste. A wooden seat covered the drain system. The seat also kept the person using it dry.

▼ There are places for twelve men to use this toilet at one time. It was built between 100 and 200 CE in Tunisia in Africa.

100–500 CE
The Romans use flush toilets and build a sewer system.

▶ This American chamber pot from the 1700s is decorated with the face of King George III.

Chamber pots

Rich Egyptians, Greeks, and Romans chose to use jars or pots as toilets. These were called **chamber pots**. Poor people simply went outside. If they were too ill to go outside, they used clay pots.

Middle Ages

During the Middle Ages (500–1450 CE), almost all flush toilets and sewer systems disappeared. People either went outside or used chamber pots.

Castles often had **garderobes**. These were small seats built into a tiny closet hanging over the castle's **moat**. Waste ran down the castle wall into the moat. Moats full of **sewage** smelled terrible.

In the 1500s, rich people used fancy chamber pots called **close stools**. Many were made to look like a box. The lid opened to show a seat decorated in velvet and lace. Beneath the seat was a pot to catch waste.

500–1450
Chamber pots and garderobes are in use. Flush toilets disappear.

1500s
Close stools are used.

1300   1400   1500

City problems

Before the 1600s, most people lived on farms or in small villages. Waste was not a problem. But as people moved to crowded cities, the problem of human waste grew. People urinated in the streets. They also emptied chamber pots onto the streets. Farmers collected some of the waste to spread on their fields as a **fertilizer**. The rest of the waste ran into rivers and **wells**. This made the water unsafe to drink.

◀ Chamber pots used to be dumped onto the street.

1600s–1800s
Cities grow and so do waste problems.

▶ This diagram shows how a toilet works. When the toilet handle is pushed, water rushes from the tank into the bowl. This forces the water and waste in the bowl to empty into the sewer drain. When the water level in the tank drains, a stopper opens. The tank refills with water.

Float ball   Float rod   Stopper   Water supply

Lever

Toilet handle

Cistern

Water

Plug

Toilet

Modern flush toilets

In 1590 English inventor Sir John Harington designed a flush toilet. He put it in his own home. A tank near the ceiling released water when the toilet's handle was pulled. Queen Elizabeth I had one set up in her palace. Few others were willing to try it. In fact, they made fun of Harington's flush toilet.

1590
English inventor
Sir John Harington
invents the flush toilet.

1738
French architect
J. F. Blondel
improves the toilet.

1600   1700

People continued to use outhouses or chamber pots until French architect J. F. Blondel made a better flush toilet in 1738. This toilet included a valve (flap) to keep odours out of the house. By the 1770s, people in Great Britain and France began putting flush toilets inside their homes. In 1870 Englishman S. S. Hellyer invented a flush toilet similar to the one people use today.

Until this time in the United States, many people did not have running water in their homes. Without running water, they could not use flush toilets. It was not until about 1870 that most US homes had indoor plumbing and flush toilets.

◀ Crapper's toilets had better flush systems than earlier toilets. This advertisement shows that they were also very decorative.

Thomas Crapper's toilet ✔

In 1884 English plumber Thomas Crapper designed a toilet that flushed more easily. Thomas Crapper & Company made many of the toilets used in Europe. Queen Victoria honoured him, but US soldiers made him famous. US soldiers working in Great Britain during World War I (1914–18) began to call toilets "crappers".

1770s	1870	1884
The British and French add indoor toilets to buildings.	Englishman S. S. Hellyer invents the modern flush toilet. Americans add indoor toilets to buildings.	English plumber Thomas Crapper improves the toilet.

1800

1900

Sewers

▲ This 1854 drawing shows workmen repairing London's Fleet Street sewer.

By the 1840s most cities had **sewer** problems. As more people used flush toilets, sewers could not handle the waste. Sewers overflowed. People became ill when **sewage** leaked into drinking water.

In London, human waste drained into the River Fleet and the River Thames. The rivers were clogged by waste, dead dogs, dead cats, and rats. Vegetables, kettles, broken pots, and all kinds of rubbish filled the sewers.

1858
London experiences "the Great Stink".

1859
London repairs its sewers.

1800   1850

The summer of 1858 was called "the Great Stink". Even members of the government left town to avoid the smell. It took years to fix the sewers. When the sewer system was finished, the stink disappeared. City dwellers then lived longer and had fewer diseases.

Sewage treatment

Even after the London sewers were repaired, waste still emptied into the River Thames. Most cities drained sewage into rivers. But human waste kills fish and clogs rivers. In 1890 some cities began to use filters and **chemicals** to treat the waste before putting it back into rivers and lakes.

In 1916 two US scientists first treated waste with **bacteria** before returning it to rivers or lakes. Many cities continue to use this system today.

Sewers of Paris

By 1878 the sewers of Paris, France, were 580 kilometres (360 miles) long. People enjoyed touring the sewers in carts pushed by workers. Later they used small trains and boats. Today, Paris's sewers cover 2,100 kilometres (1,300 miles). They remain open for tours.

▼ Tours of Paris sewers were popular in 1870, when this drawing was made.

1890
Chemicals are used to treat waste.

1916
Bacteria are used to treat waste.

1900

1950

Sewage today

People who live in the country use big tanks buried near by for sewage treatment. Waste drains from the house into these **septic tanks**. Over time, the waste breaks down. The **wastewater** flows into the ground through a **drain field**.

▶ This diagram shows how a septic system works. The scum layer breaks down into water and sludge. The system must be cleaned from time to time.

1 Waste from the home enters and divides itself into three layers.

2 The "scum layer" is anything that floats to the top.

3 The "water layer" is almost-clean water.

4 The "sludge layer" contains solid waste.

5 A pipe takes water to an underground drain field.

City and town systems

Cities and towns need larger sewer systems than septic tanks. Pipes carry waste from homes and businesses to a large pipe called a sewer main. The sewer main runs beneath the streets. Workers check the sewer mains by going down a **manhole**.

Large tanks collect waste from the sewer main. Liquid waste is separated from solid waste. Solid waste is burned or spread on farm fields as a **fertilizer**. The liquid waste is treated with a gas called chlorine and with bacteria. Then the treated waste is returned to nearby lakes and rivers.

14

Reed beds

Another system for treating wastewater is called reed-bed technology. This system uses tall grasses (called reeds) that grow in wet areas. Pipes carry sewage to the reed beds. In time the wastewater evaporates (turns into a gas). Then bacteria at the roots of the reeds break down the solid waste.

▲ This large sewage treatment plant in Munich, Germany, has many tanks for treating sewage.

Flower helpers

In 1989 National Aeronautics and Space Administration (NASA) scientists began using flowering water plants to clean wastewater. They used hyacinths, lilies, and others. Flowering plants take in waste gases and give off clean air. Later, the scientists crushed the plants and used them as fertilizer to grow corn, tomatoes, potatoes, cucumbers, and squash.

15

Cleaning up

▲ **This giant roll of paper will be made into a special kind of toilet paper for septic tanks. It breaks down about 30 seconds after flushing.**

Toilet paper was first sold in the United States in 1857. It was sold in Great Britain from about 1863. At first, people felt embarrassed about buying toilet paper. Companies sold it in plain wrappers. As time went on, toilet paper became an everyday item. Today, people would not want to live without it.

1400s
The Chinese make the first toilet paper.

1500s
Rich Europeans use paper from books for toilet paper.

1400   1500   1600

Before toilet paper

Ancient Romans used a sponge on the end of a stick to clean up after using the toilet. When finished, they put the sponge in a bucket full of water so that the next person could use it. Other early people used water to clean up. Some used stones, sand, or seashells to scrape themselves clean.

In the United States, people used corn-on-the-cobs dipped in water as toilet paper. They kept a basket of them in the outhouse. After use, they tossed the corn-on-the-cobs into the pit of the outhouse.

How much? ✔

In Europe, we use about 22 billion rolls of toilet paper a year.

The first toilet papers

The Chinese were the first to use soft toilet paper. In about 1400 CE they were making 720,000 sheets of toilet paper a year to be used by royalty. In Europe in the late 1500s, rich people took a book to the toilet. They ripped out pages to use for cleaning themselves. Poorer people used bits of paper bags, ads, and newspapers.

BEAUTIFULLY BRONZED, and Fitted with:
A ROLL OF TOILET PAPER, 67 yards long, containing 384 squares, and adjustable clip for refilling;
A BOX for MATCHES, with Striker;
A BRACKET, with Socket for LAMP or CANDLE;
A SILVERED BEVELLED MIRROR;
A RECEPTACLE FOR TOBACCO ASH, CIGAR AND CIGARETTE ENDS;
AND TOWEL HOOK.

RIPPINGILLE·BROS·PATENT

SIZE, 16 INCHES BY 10 INCHES.
Price **5/6**, Complete as drawn.
If without Lamp, and with Plain Mirror, **4s. 6d.**
Can be supplied with our special "ELEKTRON" finish, 1s. 6d. extra.

▶ **This early toilet roll holder also included a candle holder, towel hook, and mirror.**

1857
Toilet paper is sold in the United States.

1863
Toilet paper is sold in Great Britain.

1700   1800   1900

No place to go

NORTH
AMERICA

Atlantic
Ocean

Pacific
Ocean

EUROPE

ASIA

AFRICA

Indian
Ocean

SOUTH
AMERICA

AUSTRALIA

KEY

Most people have
acceptable levels
of sanitation.

Most people do not
have acceptable
levels of sanitation.

Levels of sanitation
are getting better but
exact information is
not available.

No information
is available.

 **This world map
shows the progress
of different regions
towards acceptable
levels of sanitation.**

People in Europe and North America usually take
toilets and toilet paper for granted. However, in many
parts of the world, there are not enough toilets.
Today, 2.6 billion people do not have proper toilets
and **sewer** systems.

Health dangers

Without toilets and sewer systems, human waste
may wash into nearby **wells** or streams used as
drinking water. Drinking untreated **wastewater** is
very dangerous for babies and young children. Nearly
1.6 million children under the age of five die every
year because of poor **sanitation**.

International Year of Sanitation

The United Nations (UN) made 2008 the International Year of Sanitation. One of the UN's goals is to provide safe toilets for everyone in the world by 2025. UN experts say that it will take nearly £7 billion a year to reach their goal. People in Europe spend that much on ice cream each year. Americans spend four times that much each year on their pets.

Toilet house

In 2007 a Korean lawmaker named Sim Jae-duck built a house shaped like a toilet. He called his house *Haewoojae*, which means "a place where one can solve one's worries". The house has four toilets. The one in the centre of the house is see-through. A special system fogs the glass whenever someone uses the toilet. Jae-duck built the house because he worried about the worldwide lack of proper toilets. He wants people to work on the problem.

▼ This Korean house looks like a giant toilet.

A Dutch company has designed a **urinal** that disappears beneath the street during the day. It pops up for use at night. They are in use in cities across Great Britain. The first city in North America to give the pop-ups a try is Victoria in British Columbia, Canada. By morning, the urinals are lowered beneath the street and covered with a metal cap.

Pay toilets

Where do people go to the toilet when they are away from home? Restaurants and shops sometimes have free toilets. But what if people do not want to eat or shop? Many people believe that every city and town should provide public toilets that are free, clean, and safe.

Others say that it costs too much to provide free toilets. Many European countries have public toilets in their cities. Often you have to pay to use them. The money is used to keep toilets clean and safe.

▶ It is expensive to keep public toilets clean and in good working order.

Portable toilets

Portable toilets can be delivered to where they are needed. They can be used at fairs, music festivals, and building sites. Waste collects in a tank beneath the seat. A lorry collects the waste. The lorry takes it to a **sewage** treatment plant. After the toilets are cleaned, they can be used again or moved to a new location.

▼ National parks and tourist attractions may provide portable toilets like these in Colorado, USA.

Saving water

▶ Waterless urinals like this have been in use throughout the world for a number of years.

People flush a lot of water down the toilet. In Europe and North America, most of the water used in houses is used in bathrooms. Much of the water is used for flushing. Toilets made before 1982 use between 19 and 27 litres (4.2 and 6 gallons) of water per flush. New low-flow toilets use between 4.8 and 6 litres (1 and 1.3 gallons) per flush.

Waterless urinals

Some **urinals** need no water. A waterless urinal has an odour trap made of natural vegetable oil. Since the **urine** is heavier than the oil, it passes through directly into the **sewer** system. The urinal is sprayed with a cleaner once a month. Replacing older toilets at home with these will help reduce water use.

Dual-flush toilets

Dual-flush toilets also help reduce water use. One button uses less water to flush urine. The other uses more to flush **excrement**. All new buildings in Ireland must use dual-flush toilets to save water. Australia also wants people to use dual-flush models.

Recycling toilet bowls ✔

The city of San Antonio, Texas, USA, wants citizens to buy new low-flow toilets. Since the 1990s, San Antonio has given people money towards a new toilet if they turn in water-wasting ones. The city crushes the old toilets. It uses the pieces to pave nature trails. The crushed toilet pieces reflect the light along the path at night.

◀ A dual-flush toilet has two buttons. One uses less water to flush urine. The other uses more water to flush solid waste.

23

This toilet uses gas or electricity to burn waste. It does not require any water to work.

Latrines

Lack of water is a problem throughout the world. **Latrines** work well in areas without water systems. Latrines are the most common **sanitation** system in the world. People build latrines outside by digging a deep hole and placing a support over the hole. Latrines should be far from **wells** and streams used as drinking water. Waste collects in the pit. When it is full, the pit is filled with dirt. A new latrine is dug near by. Most outhouses are latrines with covers.

Compost toilets

Compost toilets also work well in areas without a lot of water. They are sometimes used for camping, on boats, or in homes without running water. A compost toilet breaks waste down into something called humus. Humus can be spread on soil to make the soil richer for growing crops. It is safe and will not cause disease. Compost toilets cost less than flush toilets. They save water.

▼ **A compost toilet works without water or a sewer system.**

Toilets for tomorrow

▲ The International Space Station will soon use a toilet-to-tap system.

Toilets have changed in many ways over the last 4,000 years. The way people use water and treat human waste has also changed.

Recycling wastewater

About 15 cities and towns in the United States now use a "toilet-to-tap" system. It turns **wastewater** into drinking water. After the waste is treated, the water is safe to drink.

The system is used in places where there is a water shortage. It will soon be used on the International Space Station. However, it is an expensive process so would not be good for poorer countries.

Urine

Urinc is 95 per cent pure water. The other 5 per cent is made up of salt, ammonia, and other natural **chemicals**. These chemicals must be removed before urine is safe to drink. Drinking untreated urine is not safe!

Some people have rejected the idea of toilet-to-tap systems. But experts say that in time people everywhere will accept the idea of using cleaned wastewater for cooking and drinking.

Alligators? ✔

In 1935 an alligator fell off a boat into New York's East River and swam into the **sewer** system. It was captured. People began to make up frightening stories about other alligators living in the sewers.

▼ In November 2000, workers in Sydney, Australia, found this American alligator snapping turtle in the sewer. Animal experts think it was stolen from a reptile park 21 years earlier and then wandered into the sewer.

Timeline

(These dates are often approximations.)

2500 BCE
Toilets exist in Mesopotamia, the Indus Valley, and Scotland.

3000 BCE

1400s
The Chinese make the first toilet paper.

1400

1600s–1800s
Cities grow and so do waste problems.

1738
French architect J. F. Blondel improves the toilet.

1700

1884
English plumber Thomas Crapper improves and sells toilets.

1870
Englishman S. S. Hellyer invents the modern flush toilet. Americans add indoor toilets to buildings.

1863
Toilet paper is sold in Great Britain.

1890
Chemicals are used to treat waste.

1916
Bacteria are used to treat waste.

1900

This symbol shows where there is a change of scale in the timeline, or where a long period of time with no noted events has been left out.

2000 BCE
Flush toilets are used in Crete.

2000 BCE   **1000** BCE

500–1450
Chamber pots and **garderobes** are in use. Flush toilets disappear.

100–500 CE
The Romans use flush toilets and build a **sewer** system.

1000 CE   **0**

1500s
Rich Europeans use paper from books as toilet paper. **Close stools** are used.

1500

1590
English inventor Sir John Harington invents the flush toilet.

1600

1770s
The British and French add indoor toilets to buildings.

1859
London repairs its sewers.

1858
London experiences "the Great Stink".

1857
Toilet paper is sold in the United States.

1800

1982
Low-flow toilets are widely available.

2008
The United Nations sponsors the International Year of **Sanitation**.

2025
The United Nations hopes to meet world sanitation needs by this date.

2000

Glossary

bacterium (more than one: **bacteria**) tiny living thing that can be used to treat sewage. Some bacteria cause disease, but others are used to treat sewage.

BCE meaning "before the common era". When this appears after a date, it refers to the time before the Christian religion began. BCE dates are always counted backwards.

CE meaning "common era". When this appears after a date, it refers to the time after the Christian religion began.

chamber pot jug or pot used as a toilet. Some chamber pots were simple, but others had fancy decorations.

chemical something used to remove dangerous germs from wastewater. Chemicals help treat sewage.

close stool fancy kind of chamber pot used by the wealthy in the 1500s. The seats of close stools featured decorations in fine materials such as velvet and lace.

drain field area of soil surrounding a septic tank. The drain field soaks up liquid waste from the septic tank.

excrement waste matter discharged from the body. Sewage treatment plants separate excrement from liquid waste.

fertilizer something that makes soil produce better crops. It is safe to use human waste as fertilizer.

garderobe toilet built into the wall of a castle that drained into the moat. Garderobes were cold and drafty in winter.

latrine trench dug into the ground and used as a toilet. During wars, soldiers build latrines near their camps.

manhole covered opening in the street that leads to sewer pipes. Workers climb down manholes to check the sewers.

moat water surrounding a castle. In the past, people in castles drained sewage into the moat.

sanitation method of dealing with human waste or sewage. Everyone in the world needs good sanitation.

septic tank system for treating waste in areas without sewer systems. Some people who live in the country use septic tanks.

sewage human waste. Sewage goes through pipes into the sewer system.

sewer pipe used for carrying away sewage. Most cities and towns have a sewer system.

urinal toilet used for liquid waste that is attached to a wall. Urinals are found in men's toilets.

urine liquid human waste. Urine is mainly made up of water.

wastewater water that has been used for washing, flushing, or in manufacturing; also called sewage. Wastewater must be treated at a sewage treatment plant before it is returned to rivers or lakes.

well hole dug in the earth in order to get water. Sewage should be kept away from wells.

Find out more

Books

Getting to Know Your Toilet: The Disgusting Story Behind Your Home's Strangest Feature, Connie C. Miller (Capstone Press, 2009)

The Human Machine: Digestion and Excretion, Louise Spilsbury (Heinemann Library, 2008)

Wastewater, Sally Morgan (Smart Apple Media, 2007)

Websites

Visit the website of the International Year of Sanitation.
http://esa.un.org/iys/

Visit the website of the Museum of Toilets.
www.sulabhtoiletmuseum.org/pg01.htm

Read about the history of toilets from the ancient world to the present day.
www.localhistories.org/toilets.html

Learn more about decorated toilets.
www.victoriancrapper.com

Places to visit

Visit your city's or town's water department. You may be able to tour the sewer system.

Index